Inscriptions of the Heart

Inscriptions of the Heart

A Poetic Journey through the Rough
and Joyous Places of the Soul

Brittney Balfour

Foreword by Lewin Mayers

RESOURCE *Publications* • Eugene, Oregon

INSCRIPTIONS OF THE HEART
A Poetic Journey through the Rough and Joyous Places of the Soul

Copyright © 2022 Brittney Balfour. All rights reserved. Except for brief quotations in critical publications or reviews, no part of this book may be reproduced in any manner without prior written permission from the publisher. Write: Permissions, Wipf and Stock Publishers, 199 W. 8th Ave., Suite 3, Eugene, OR 97401.

Resource Publications
An Imprint of Wipf and Stock Publishers
199 W. 8th Ave., Suite 3
Eugene, OR 97401

www.wipfandstock.com

PAPERBACK ISBN: 978-1-6667-3381-5
HARDCOVER ISBN: 978-1-6667-2876-7
EBOOK ISBN: 978-1-6667-2877-4

JANUARY 7, 2022 10:25 AM

Dedicated to those that are brave enough to be vulnerable

Contents

Foreword by LEWIN MAYERS | *xi*

Acknowledgements | *xiii*

NATURE

Ruach | 3

Alone | 4

Fall Ache | 5

The Autumn Tree | 6

Summer | 7

His Love like Snow | 8

White as Snow | 9

Unbothered | 10

Fallen | 11

Sunset | 12

Night | 13

Brohm Lake | 14

The Beach | 15

People & Relationships

Words | 19

Half-Way | 20

Clay | 21

Heart Turmoil | 22

My Validation | 23

Risk Taker | 24

Goodbyes | 25

My Jonathan | 26

You | 27

Before Its Time | 28

Chaos | 29

History | 30

Mind Battles

Restless Mind | 33

Hallmark Fantasies | 34

Plagued | 35

Insomnia | 36

No Longer | 37

Hope & Faith

In the Middle | 41

Loss | 42

Hope | 43

Romans 8:18 | 44

Eden | 45

Anchor | 46

The Waiting | 47

He Who Commands the Clouds | 48

The Sparrow | 49

Broken | 50

One | 51

Fighting for Us | 52

Overthrown | 53

Elijah's Prayer | 54

Your Walls in Ruins | 55

Defender | 56

I Hope You Dance | 57

Foreword

BRITTNEY BALFOUR has been writing and reciting poems from early childhood. All the indicators signaled to us then that she was born with the unique gift, possessing an observant and expressive heart. She retained a quiet spirit that views, listens, interprets, and responds to life in its varied dimensions and movements from an uncommon frame.

Like a true word-artist, her paintbrushes are the keys on her keyboard, and her paints are those specially coined phrases, birthed within her heart and expressed in her work. So that her poems may be likened to inspired tapestry, interwoven with patterns of metaphor, emotion, rhyme, mood, form, intrigue, and invitations for action. I have always admired her meticulous approach to crafting and reciting her poems, with a storyteller's appeal. She knows well how to capture the moment and can easily contextualize events to make them relatable to others.

As a scholar, she studied in the field of Literature and Linguistics, and applies her training to broaden the scope of her writings. She is a committed believer who loves the Lord and is actively involved in fulfilling the Great Commission.

As you read this book, you will confirm that the author writes from a depth of knowledge and awareness of life, which far surpasses her chronological age. You will be enthralled by themes that envelope issues of the heart, faith, hope, relationships, nature, and the mind. You will soon discover that you are in the poems; that they are your stories. For truth be told, there are so many issues in life that are common to mankind.

I do believe that you will be all the better in heart and mind from reading and sharing this book.

LEWIN MAYERS
Pastor, Counsellor and Lecturer

Acknowledgements

I AM THANKFUL TO GOD for the vision he placed in my heart many years ago; for his promises that are always yes and amen for those of us who would believe. For the family and friends that believed I had something special to offer to the world, thank you for your faith. For those of you that were willing to endorse my work as a new writer, I am honored that you would do so. A special thank you to my friend Sophia who worked with me late into the night to help edit my poems; your input was invaluable. And for those of you who have decided to join me on this journey of the heart, I am especially grateful for you. May you see that we bear the same scars and can find the same healing and grace.

Nature

Ruach

Breath of God from the mouth of the lake
And the mountain heights blow
Rise up from the thick of the trees
Come sweetly and blow on my face
Then inside of me go deep and heal
Those broken places and hurts
Breathe and blow and make me new
Fill me through and through
Oh mighty wind arrest my soul
Lest I never be made whole.

Alone

Twigs break beneath my feet as I walk the path,
The bleak sky presses upon my mood,
The birds in their corners sing a melancholy tune.
The river is still,
The trees are barren,
The path forsaken,
There is no one around.

I walk with my hands sagging to the side,
There is no one to hold them,
The clouds are angry fists that condemn.
The rain falls,
The snow melts,
The path is soggy,
There is no one around.

I look between the bushes and a rabbit scurries by,
Not even he has time to peek,
Daunted by absence, tears fall from my cheek.
The sun rises,
The mountains gleam,
The waters recede,
God comes down.

Fall Ache

I watched as the colored leaves fell from the tree,
And I knew my time will soon come to leave.
They littered the river, floating on its bed,
And I wondered about life and where it has led.

I looked at the tree and felt a sadness for its loss,
Yet sturdy and firm, it held no such remorse.
Release was part of its life's journey,
But I could see in letting go, no hint of glory.

The wind blew, scattering beauty with its breath,
Down in spiral waves, to the dryness of death.
Some landed at my feet, on the firm sand,
And my heart ached as a pilgrim in this majestic land.

Upward glared the sun, a large diamond in the sky,
And I remembered that joy still could be mine.
For though in one season, we may lose,
God always restores, refines and soothes.

For he knows well how to wield joy and gladness,
From the dark, cold tides of pain and sadness.
He invites us to let some good things die,
So that to life and purpose we can steadily stride.

The tree held wisdom, beyond the scope of my years—
To trap winter's moisture, none could be spared.
And though my will was still unyielding,
My feet took the path of the joyfully wounded.

The Autumn Tree

Once he wore a heavy, jeweled crown,
Now it flies scantily in the open, crisp air,
His diamonds wind downwards slowly from his head,
Dancing to the rhythm of a gentle, fleeting song.

He knows what we cannot perceive,
That true life comes from our ability to sever,
Those things that once may have brought us pleasure,
His bough now barren, emptied to heal.

Emboldened, he stands, in seasonal starkness,
Beauty, he understands, takes many forms,
Though the eyes of the onlooker may mourn,
For the winter to come, he takes on this likeness.

Oh, that we might stand just as gallant,
In our season of shedding and tears,
God had not designed it for our despair,
But to help us grow and triumph.

Summer

Gentle breeze teasing the clammy skin
Bare backs, goldened, beneath the sun's glint
Fresh water brushed by the boat's big bow
Giddy laughter streaming from loud lips.

Tired minds, beneath the trees drifting
Juveniles, the hidden ale tasting
Feet freed, frolic on the trail of escape
Reality a prison to flee.

Eyes flicker in mutual awareness
The heart is drawn in summer's wildness
Dreams are again a scented flower
Hope, the unveiled, stretching horizon.

Oh the wind of summer will soon end
And the heart exposed will hurt again.

His Love like Snow

White, thick flurries,
Burying the rooftops,
Weighing down the tree limbs,
Blanketing the fields,
Steadily coming,
Overtaking,
Everything around,
Consumed wholly I am.

White as Snow

Manna cascades from heaven
In showers of gentle snow
The earth by bliss imprisoned
My heart aches to know—

A purity so marked and pristine
That purges the darkened soul
A mind so recklessly serene
That shakes the human whole.

I dance in the dripping glory
For looking back, I've found
A crimson flow that made all white
Oh, I'm no longer bound.

The white drops tumble and fall
And I savor the implicit law
That a mind sullied by lust and gore
Can with mercy, be snowed upon.

Unbothered

By the river I come, I sit and write,
Hidden from the world's sorrowful din,
I gaze intently at the shimmering waters,
Finding warmth within.

The sun touches my right cheek,
The birds whisper a conspiracy,
Children scamper in the near distance,
Framing the rustic beauty—

Of tall, bony trees, with hungry limbs outstretched,
Dotted lines guarding the edge of the shores,
The sky a lofty banner of blue,
Sponged with white cotton balls.

The snow-capped mountains raise their heads,
Stretching to kiss the horizon,
Heaven seems perfect, as I gaze upward,
All is good and delightful.

Here the gentle waters whisper
An encrypted message—
Only a detached soul
Can come away unburdened.

Fallen

Broken earth, now cracked and bare
Once lush and fair, now withered
Thorns and briers, its common wear
The sound of war comes hither.

Eden once, now dark and cold
Peace and grace have fled
Mighty warrior, bent down low
All of earth has bled.

That power was never its own
A message now sounded clear
The created should not take the throne
Oh here's a tale to tell.

Now a dreary abode in anguish
But its creator has his ways
Though by its deeds now ravished
Broken earth shall be replaced.

Sunset

Soft, pastel strokes, sweep across the sky,
A canvas of quiet glory, erupts before my eyes,
The mountains sit in cheery-like glow,
And my soul, whispers, Abba . . .
I find myself a child at ease,
Sitting on your lap,
You stretch my knotted coils of hair,
I giggle contentedly, without fear.
A dream of a kind, gentle father,
Morphs out of the soft, candied dusk,
I snatch all of peace, for it is mine,
I become, as I behold.

Night

The mighty forest below, absorbed
By the pressing, seeking darkness,
Night critters whistle their eerie tune,
The wind's breath, chilling the earth.

The lake so foreboding 'neath the sun,
Now smothered in obscurity,
The mountains so grand at day's yawn,
Reduced by dark's invasion.

The clouds pass over the glowing stars,
And I wonder about the prevailing darkness,
That everything is devoured by its force,
Bound by creation's, timeless, oath.

But morning will again soon raise its head,
Releasing night's tortured victims,
Hope will march o'er the horizon,
Breaking dark's damning dominion.

And though night descends with a gripping hold,
Grace will burst forth, at day's threshold.

Brohm Lake

Life flows in swirling patterns
Creating a pool of beauty
Tiny, gentle ripples glisten
Growing silver, before the eyes.

The tall pine trees, stand stately by
Guarding the great, wide shores
Whispers of majesty echo around
Immanuel is present.

He who churns the deep
And commands the sweeping tide
It is he that stands above the lake
Spinning life into existence.

Oh, living water, that from his hands spill
Though the lake be glorious, his presence is more still.

The Beach

Salt-dusted waves climb high
Beauty foaming at their crest
Curling, crashing and taking
Undaunted by the rest

The monstrous depth of water
So ominous in its speech
Enclosed in my heart and mind
Is a picture of the beach

The islands curve around it
Forested little heaps
Skylight streaks down its dark pit
Causing the eye to weep

Men gather in little clusters
Basking upon the shore
Feet brave, dare to wander
Beneath the tidal floor.

Though far beyond I've traveled
Upon desert and dry land
Always pointing to home
Is a marriage of water and sand.

People & Relationships

Words

I invited your words into my story
And it broke through my reality
My soul, an ember, that threatens to die
All from the words that you said.

Destiny now a fearsome road
For what was dreamt, now has no hold
Fairytales lost and desires faded
All from the words that you said.

Beauty ran thither, miles away
Glory escaped another way
Neither possessed this frame of mine
All from the words that you said.

Yet, what sorrow to let your words define
What sadness to claim them all as mine
When another has spoken and given me life
All from the words that He said.

Half-Way

Praise, tumbled from my lips
But yours remained muted
Longing dripped from my eyes
But yours were diluted.

Poetry, spilled from my hands
I painted you with words
I ran towards the half-way mark
But you stood there unperturbed.

I shivered in grasping the open truth
That love was not coming my way
I had rushed to meet you half-way
But purpose had its own say.

Clay

Oh, earthly thing, carved from dust,
It is you that I yearn for, to give my full trust.
Touched with a smudge of divinity,
You bear the marks of the eternal,
But your days are all numbered,
Your frame will become frail,
Wisdom beckons me to look away.
I'm bound to lose my way, if I'm so inclined,
To make an idol from what will die,
I must put you in your rightful place,
For thou art not the potter but only the clay.

Heart Turmoil

Water seeking to push through the cracks
As such is my pressed, bulging heart
His eyes, his eyes, his shaded lashed eyes
Emotions once buried, now risen.

Hurt peeks its head o'er the sharp horizon
Rejection glances through the gray clouds
My soul, can harbor but a morsel of faith
In the dark, secret place of the hidden.

Oh to trust the hand of the savior
With these fragile heart concerns
His strength invades our weaknesses
As we tarry and wait for the sudden.

Still, his eyes meet mine, in quick exchange
I crave to partake in the soul's sacred dance
Yet my troubled will I tearfully submit
In the lure of the great forbidden.

My Validation

It comes not from drawn up fantasies—
Holding hands or laughing in reverie
Where the world can see us together
Or a dream of us, pledged for forever

Nor diminished by your lack of contact
Or truncated by some hearsay fact
Nor reduced by your lack of calls
Or impoverished by your building up of walls

These things will not change my worth
Stamped was I, with glory, before birth
Oh, your deeds cannot put to the sickle
What God has ordained, in my cradle.

Risk Taker

He bids you come on water,
Weak feet with boldness dip
Into the fearsome unknown,
Where sacrifice is sown.

Daring the path less taken,
You bravely forge ahead,
Holding the savior's hand,
Breaking covenant with dry land.

A vision, stands before you tall—
That all be saved, none lost,
Blinded men deride your choice,
But you will not this burden toss.

Goodbyes

Tears inflict my brown face,
Anguish, a heavy cross,
Another embrace loosened,
Another moved miles away,
Waving hands, a distant memory.

Oh change, that twists the heart
Into a deep, dreary abyss,
I dwell there in loneliness,
I dwell there in pain,
Hurt tucked inside and buried.

The sun wakes and melts the cold,
And I remember a steadfast love,
It never dwindles,
It never disappears,
Yet goodbyes are tombs we carry.

My Jonathan

Who has tarried with me on this journey?
Remaining faithful, despite the grime—
Of festered wounds, from hidden trauma,
Of immature lips and insecure banter.

Who has walked this path of bliss?
Of two souls growing together,
Tickled laughter and secrets shared,
Unfettered honesty many would fear.

It is you, my friend, that truly knows,
The insanity of true friendship,
That herein lies an abiding covenant
Our souls cannot forfeit.

Though life may grow inconsistent,
Our bond would throughout remain,
A loyalty, that would guard our lineage,
A love, that would in all things, prevail.

You

My eyes narrow upon your image,
All others I can see walking as trees,
Your poise, your gait, your smile,
I am gripped with want.

Peace escapes the turbulent heart,
Rejection stalks the broken soul,
Timidly I creep near desire's door,
But the answer remains no.

Yet a closed door has no power,
Though the pain be intensely sharp,
If we look at it as God's reminder
That he is working out our path.

Though I want to stroke your hair,
I humbly take my bow,
For love is not always fair,
Yet despair will not be my resolve.

Before Its Time

By the gazelles of the field,
You spoke your demand,
Love shouldn't be aroused,
Till its time is at hand.

But I shook it wide awake,
In the pains of deep desire,
Though sin came crouching by,
I wanted to enquire.

Oh premature and ailing,
It could not last long,
Sudden and impulsive crazes,
Not the full note of Solomon's song.

So I'll wait for the appointed time,
When grace is there to love,
For my heart had paid a terrible fine,
I was not so easily absolved.

Chaos

I opened wide another door,
No thought for what will come,
I flung it open, careless and free,
Letting every foul thing in.
The ground jolted,
Darkness ensued,
The door slammed shut,
I became trapped on the inside.

History

Here in a land of histories, I wonder of my own,
Of generations gone by, and seeds once sown.
Had I been hewn from a rock of precious stones?
Or emerged from a lineage full of woes?

What happened before I nestled in my mother's womb?
The many secrets embalmed in my ancestral tomb.
My roots are dust particles, that mingle and disperse,
Traces are absent, a road not traversed.

I'm a fragment, in a nation tied by ancestry,
Whose past is connected to their destiny.
Perhaps one day, I will discover my story,
And share the joy of those who know their history.

Mind Battles

Restless Mind

Quiet thyself, oh frenzied mind,
Let go of the gnawing past,
Dig not up those ruthless thoughts,
For your redeemer is strong.

Grab not those wild images,
That shake passion wide awake,
Free thyself and look ahead,
For your redeemer is strong.

Tarry not in the dark of the night,
What good can musing do?
Sojourn not to that place once sweet,
For your redeemer is strong.

Drag with might, thy restlessness,
And tether it to the cross,
Oh peace can only be found
In your redeemer who is strong.

Hallmark Fantasies

Trapped in pitiful reverie,
I childishly pursue,
Dreams of us holding hands,
Beneath the sky's reddish blue.

Thoughts that are most endearing,
Trickle through my mind,
Seemingly harmless, hallmark trinkets,
Mistletoe and Christmas pine.

But I bear the marks of the sufferer,
That escape the bore of reality,
Wrapped in the frill of illusion,
I subtly lose my sobriety.

Maybe one day you will kiss my head,
Under the snow drenched sky,
But abiding here with a heart unguarded,
Would leave me impoverished by lies.

Plagued

I rejoice in the fitful nights
That make me cling to thee
That bid this pen to do its work
My heavy soul, upward, to look

Shaken and tired, I cannot trace
These troubled, toxic thoughts
Oh, that you would soon deliver
If not, I will praise and remember—

That darkness will not for long prevail
And life will have us sometimes travail.

Insomnia

Oh my soul, be at rest,
From the things that plague thee so,
For every problem be earth-bound,
Though stress be a cumbersome foe.

Why feast on such uncertain things,
That bears but a semblance of truth?
For chaos breeds insanity,
Producing no good fruit.

Each problem crumbles in the eternal's face,
For the sovereign Lord comes with power,
To cast aside all earthly threat,
That may seek to devour.

So rest and dwell, oh fitful mind,
May it thus be said,
That He gives good sleep to his beloved,
And only peace can shake hell.

No Longer

Scattered thoughts, worry and hurt
Make haste and flee

Oh daunting shadow, that stalked from birth
No longer dwell with me

Have you not seen, the sturdy mountain
That sits on the river's bed?

Have you not seen, the mighty trees
Where birds and creatures dwell?

Then you have seen the maker's imprint
For strength and wonder are his

You have seen the healer's hand
For darkness he turns to bliss

No longer are you welcome
You have no right to reign

Linger hence no further
For God's right hand will sustain.

Hope & Faith

In the Middle

Tousled by life's uncertainties,
Its twists, bends and curves,
Fear's indignant grasp on tomorrow,
Overshadowing love, in the middle.

Fierce and ruthless with contempt,
Ploughing and turning hearts,
Death's damning curse on tomorrow,
Choking promise, here in the middle.

But in the middle stood he crucified,
While everything seemed misplaced,
Victory's steeled foot on tomorrow,
Trampling sorrow, here in the middle

And in the middle of every struggle,
I will not yield to despair,
For he who parts the middle,
Will bring my freedom near.

Loss

Expectation, in the soul's womb, miscarried,
What I hoped for, was now buried,
The morning came but without the sun,
By night, my peace was undone.

I waited in the aged room of prayer,
Yet joy was dim and seldom there,
My seed of hope, now swept away,
Into the realm of the forgotten laid.

My eyes could not behold the promise,
Sacred dreams ruefully relinquished,
But in the place of confusion, I understand,
That God in his sovereignty still has a plan.

Perhaps my season is yet to come,
I must look up, where my help comes from,
So I shake in frustration, but then rest in his will,
For one day, that expectation he may again fulfill.

And if never, because he has something different,
In his grace I will live and not die in the present.

Hope

The sun's rays caress my face,
I can feel destiny's tug,
Eyes fixed and heart yielded,
My face extends upward.

Past aches and future fears
Are swallowed up in hope,
I ponder 'pon the path ordained,
As I bask 'neath heaven's hood.

Peace hovers o'er my heart,
Love beckons my tired feet,
Emmanuel's face I behold,
Till I am no longer bothered.

I dare to hope again,
As I look upon the light,
Oh days like this come seldom,
But for now, I am unfettered.

Romans 8:18

The toils and strains of a broken heart,
The wounds left from a rotten path,
The aches and trials of each new day,
The tiredness of feet, trying to find their way,
The groans and ills of a world filled with pain,
The loneliness that comes from the onslaught of rain,

None can compare with the glory to come,
When death will be completely strung,
And every doleful thing that on earth persists,
Be thrown for eternity into the blazing abyss,
And our frail bodies, infirmities, and sinful minds,
Unto Eden's wholeness, forever, be made reconciled.

Oh, if we hold fast to this day of promise,
In times severe, we can have great solace.

Eden

Shalom shaken; the command forsaken
O'er the lie that delight was kept hidden

Grace squandered; favor forgotten
On the winds of memories dark and forbidden

Heart hardened; a plea to harken
Denied by the soul, so reckless and maddened

A broken place we find ourselves
Till our hearts are ploughed and we make amends

Till then he woos us by his grace
Wounded hands wait for the broken to gently embrace.

Anchor

Let my soul anchor to thee
As these stormy gales bellow
Avert my eyes from the raging sea
Lest I be hung in despair's gallows.

Though peril draws near
Let me sojourn at your feet
Though the darkness brings fear
Give your beloved sweet sleep.

Oh dust that I am, frail and torn
Anchor me in your love and truth
Be my strength when I am worn
That I may always abide in the root.

Fail me not, though the night is at hand
Cause my feet through all to stand.

The Waiting

Thick puffs of clouds frame its beauty
As I fix my eyes upon the glorious heavens,
I learn to trust in your sovereignty,
Here in the waiting.

Time passes like the cool wind,
Plans hoped for, not yet birthed,
This season, a sick tree, barren,
Here I am in the waiting.

I hunger still for your word,
I wait for you to come close,
I sit silent till your voice is heard,
Here in the waiting.

I open myself to your grace,
I learn, I write, I pray,
Your assurance drips like rain,
Here in the waiting.

They drip onto the dry sod of my heart,
Breaking open seeds of faith,
Be strong and courageous, along the path,
Words echoed, in the waiting.

In these wilted seasons that appear,
I drag my feet outdoors to stand,
I behold your glory and drown fear,
You surround me in the waiting.

He Who Commands the Clouds

Scattered clouds amass together,
My tattered self becoming whole,
For he who commands the clouds,
Will nurture my weary soul,

His hands are not too short,
That he couldn't reach my dirt,
His power not too weak,
He couldn't qualify my worth,

I look up and I gaze,
Who among all else is mighty?
I lie down and I rest,
Who else can bring the victory?

Ride on the clouds and come,
Oh Lord, leave me wholly undone.

The Sparrow

The common bird receives his grace
Each one under his watchful gaze

Not one will fall, lest he but know
Yet fear for our lives, we daily show

Are not two sold for a careless penny?
Yet we wonder about our life's journey

We wonder if God would come through and provide
If the same God that subtracts, can also multiply

We wrestle with thoughts of his perfect care
Yet he numbers each strand of hair

If to the sparrow he gives his full attention
How much more on us would he lavish his affection?

Oh, the lowly sparrow receives his part
But we receive his very heart.

Broken

A broken jar of clay I am,
That grace only and only grace can bind.

Wounded and scarred, traumas unfold,
Triggers abound in the mind's hellish hole.

Yet hands deeply pierced have borne my fears,
A body impaled, the pain of my years.

Now let peace and love like a bursting dam,
Gush forth from this barren land.

Oh grace that holds this vessel of mine,
Come seep through and refine.

Let every wound be to thy praise,
And every scar, a divine trace.

One

Noise fades into the periphery,
The heart is now ready to listen,
The cares of this world crumble,
Sweet communion breaks open.
The peace of God falls
In gentle whispers of truth,
The weary soul unladen.

Something has manifested,
A love, in chaos, unknown,
A heart erupts with laughter,
A father's touch rests tender.
Fears absorb in faith,
Lips spill forth praise,
God and man are one.

Fighting for Us

Despair, in dark shadows, falls
Our knees again hit the floor
Your banner still raised as the battle soars
You stand armed for us like you did before.

Though disease and pain stomp the earth
Our eyes rest on redemption's hill
Where angels stand ready to avert
Every act outside your sovereign will.

Our hearts now sifted, for you we yearn
You bring grief, but will show us compassion
For our cause you have not grown unconcerned
Against hell you'll raise an insurrection.

Overthrown

The King of glory from his throne reigns
Though the fires of hell spill forth and blaze
His greatness defies sickness and pain
Death's choke on the saint has no real claim

Though trouble, like an angry foe, comes raging
Blessed are those, who for redemption are waiting
And the heart that be locked up by hurt and misery
Knows that one day, it shall be fetter-free

For when he steps in and takes control
Every power there is will be overthrown.

Elijah's Prayer

In that still, small voice, come speak to me
When I am not where I ought to be
In my anger and weakness, come tend to my soul
Take the broken pieces and make them whole.

Touch me in the wilderness, when I am too weak
Nudge me with your hand, when death is all I speak
Ask me and ask me again, "Why I am here?"
Till I come face to face with my present fear.

Come by the cave, where I stand, listening to your voice
Give me your direction, so I can make the right choice
Woo me by your spirit, with angelic love and care
Whenever I'm on the run from life, sweet savior draw me near.

Your Walls in Ruins

I cannot bear your agony,
Your trampled, withered face,
Your heart, a dirge-like melody,
As you sit in silent rage.

But I will rebuild your walls,
Though you be hurt and tarnished,
I will heal your flaws,
My mighty hand will quickly salvage.

I have never lost sight of your ruins,
Though you've lost sight of my hand,
I've seen all their evil doings,
I will restore, and I can.

In your desert place, lonely and dry,
I will hold your tears in my hand,
Believe not the enemy's lie,
I will cause your weak feet to stand.

Can a mother feel no love for her child?
Even if such a wretched thing takes place,
I will never forget you are mine,
Nor your ruins, and your need for my grace.

Defender

Troubled heart, laden with despair,
Your advocate sits high, but draws near,
To your stilted cry, choked with pain,
To your brokenness, your inward shame.

He lifts your head, brushing off your ashes,
Every dark stain, he carefully washes,
His hand with force strikes your enemy,
And erases injustice with bold dexterity.

So gather the crumbs of your failing hope,
In your weakness, he will make his abode.
Look up dear child here comes your defender,
He will be to you a mighty warrior.

I Hope You Dance

In the swirling madness,
Let your body tremble with praise,
Feet stomping, hands waving
Toward the throne of grace.

For in your sadness, racked with tears,
Let the tambourine and drums be heard,
Graceful lifting, back bent shaking,
Let your soul declare his word.

I hope you dance; I pray you dance,
Till the shackles that bind you fall,
I hope you dance; I pray you dance,
Till peace consumes your all.

And in thy broken place,
Joy will come and overtake,
If you would just but move,
Healing will soon break.

www.ingramcontent.com/pod-product-compliance
Lightning Source LLC
Chambersburg PA
CBHW061510040426
42450CB00008B/1545